MW0071125?

STEP OUTSIDE

URBAN TERRACES & BALCONIES

STEP OUTSIDE
URBAN TERRACES & BALCONIES

ÀLEX SÁNCHEZ VIDIELLA

LOFT

STEP OUTSIDE. URBAN TERRACES & BALCONIES

Editorial Coordinator: Simone K. Schleifer
Assistant to Editorial Coordination: Aitana Lleonart
Editor and Texts: Àlex Sánchez Vidiella

Art Director: Mireia Casanovas Soley
Design and Layout Coordination: Claudia Martínez Alonso
Layout: Anabel N. Quintana

Projects: Arboretum – www.arboretum.es
Images: Jordi Jové – www.jordi-jove.com
Styling: Ilang Paz – www.ilangpaz.com
          Dplata-estilismos – www.dplata.com
Staging: www.jacaredobrasil.es
          www.luzio.es
          www.boconcept.es

English Translation: Cillero & de Motta

© 2009 Loft Publications

ISBN: 978-84-92463-92-3

Loft Publications wishes to give special thanks to the
Arboretum team and Jordi Jové for their contributions of
graphical material, their collaboration and their invaluable
assistance when this book was being drafted.

All rights reserved. No part of this book may be used or reproduced
in any manner whatsoever without written permission except in the
case of brief quotations embodied in critical articles and reviews.

INDEX ....

INTRODUCTION

City dwellers often buy or rent properties and pay a premium for a garden so they can have direct access to their own highly prized 'private outdoors space'.

Surely any open space in the city is a great bonus, however small. And these days, creating a fabulous outdoor plot doesn't require you to become a horticulture guru.

Whether you're looking to employ a professional at certain steps of the way or have a go at it yourself, a successful garden will need time, focus, and creativity. The more technical and often structural issues will probably need an expert, but ideas and inspiration are everywhere. Visiting other gardens will fill you with ideas about layouts and planting. Local gardens will also show you which plants will thrive in your immediate area. Look beyond gardens too as ideas can come from many other sources; art, public landscape, architecture can often trigger valuable concepts and help stimulate interesting designs.

You'll certainly need to get your head round budgets but there's nothing better to spend your money on, knowing that this investment should be quickly add value to the property.

Joe Swift
Garden Designer, TV Presenter and Writer

ROOFTOP LUXURY

FLOORING/PAVING: Gray wood-polymer composite (WPC) decking.

PLANT POTS AND PLANTER BOXES: Charcoal gray rotomolded polyethylene (PE) plant pots.

FURNISHINGS: Chill out sofa in gray WPC, cushions covered in marine-grade fabric, anodized aluminum and PE side table, Phantom Chair.

PLANT SPECIES: *Thuja aurea* and *Buxus sempervirens rotundifolia*.

LIGHTING: Stainless steel recessed bi-pin spotlights, bi-pin die cast aluminum halogen spotlights.

Access to the roof terrace of this detached single-family home is through the master bedroom. Its location at the highest point of the building gives enables its owners to enjoy magnificent views while protecting their privacy. The couple's luxurious bedroom was already complete with a gymnasium and a wet zone containing a spa bath, sauna, and a relaxing shower, so the designers decided that the main use of the terrace would be as a solarium. No canopies or awnings were built in this space so that the central area of the terrace would remain clear. This design allowed the sunloungers to be positioned and moved at will, depending on the sun.

WPC boards were used in the decking and the furniture as this material barely needs maintenance and practically does not deteriorate. The farthest part of the terrace from the bedroom has an L-shaped sofa where the sun can be enjoyed while one is reading or having a refreshing drink. A number of plant pots are visible on a bed of marble pebbles.

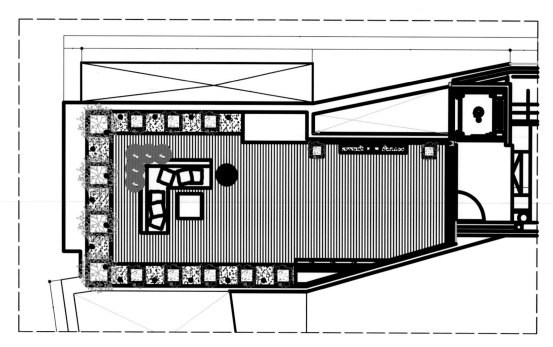

Recessed spotlights were installed in the floor to illuminate the plant pots. A number of the spotlights are also directed at the trees to create a warm atmosphere at night that can be felt from inside the bedroom.

A two-level fixture with a gray finish was built on one of the ends. It serves several purposes, such as a side table for food service, a bar, and shelves to hold towels.

One step separates the house from this dream space, where you can almost touch the sky.

SEA VIEWS

FLOORING/PAVING: Autoclave-treated Flanders pine, walnut stained.

FURNISHINGS: Rotomolded PE deck chair. Rotomolded PE ottoman and table with light.

PLANT SPECIES: *Citrus limon, Buxus sempervirens rotundifolia,* and *Pittosporum tobira nana.*

LIGHTING: Die-cast aluminum halogen spotlights.

A new use was decided for this natural terrace forming part of the hotel grounds by merging the hotel and nature in the one space. A zone for relaxation and massage was created to enable hotel guests to contemplate the wonderful sea views while bathing or receiving a massage. In order to level the uneven terrain, pine wood decking was laid. Three pergolas were also built of the same material with square-section crossbeams and supports. These pergolas are staggered rather than arranged parallel to each other. Inside the space created is a spa bath, and also a number of massage beds and three relaxing showers separated by wooden partitions.

Several wooden fixtures were also built of the same wood for use by hotel staff. Marble shelves provide storage for towels and support for ceramic basins. Simple cotton curtains between the pergolas offer the privacy needed for this type of service.

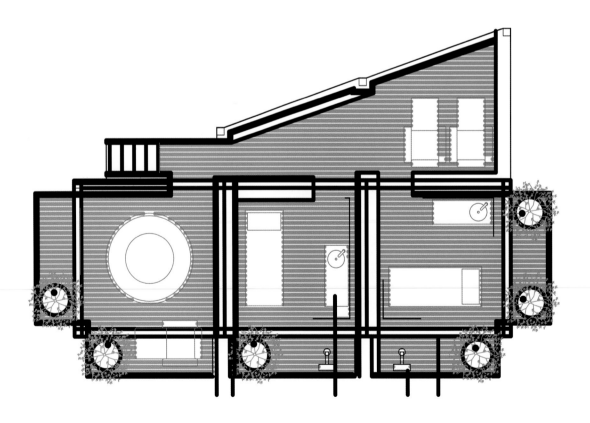

The owners of the hotel wanted to give a specific use to the area of the grounds between the rooms and the swimming pool. The result was the creation of a relaxation space featuring pine pergolas.

THE SENSES ARE IMBUED WITH TRANQUILITY WHILE THE LIGHT GLINTING OFF THE SEA FILTERS THROUGH THE SHEER CURTAINS.

MAGICAL NIGHTS

FLOORING/PAVING: Gray WPC decking.

PLANT POTS AND PLANTER BOXES: Plant pots in charcoal gray rotomolded PE and plant pots in white rotomolded PE with light.

FURNISHINGS: Sofa, ottoman and table in rotomolded PE.

PLANT SPECIES: *Citrus limon*, *Buxus sempervirens rotundifolia*, and *Pittosporum tobira nana*.

LIGHTING: Die-cast aluminum halogen spotlights, rotomolded PE plant pots and furniture with light, and rotomolded PE Ciprés (cypress) lamp.

The terrace of this luxury home practically surrounds the entire apartment. To give the setting a feel of elegance, gray WPC was used as decking. The walls were designed in the same material. The low density of the WPC strips provided increased natural light entering the interior and improved ventilation. This design gives the terrace great importance and all of the rooms in the apartment are open to it.

Different varieties of plants were arranged strategically; their placement next to the windows of each room also allows the terrace to be enjoyed from inside. Additionally, in order to break the regular pattern produced by the "wooden" strips, square zones were created using white marble pebbles. These "white rugs" change the direction of the floor boards and break the somber nature of the design. The idea of including and outdoor eating area on the terrace was ruled out; instead, this space was created for relaxation.

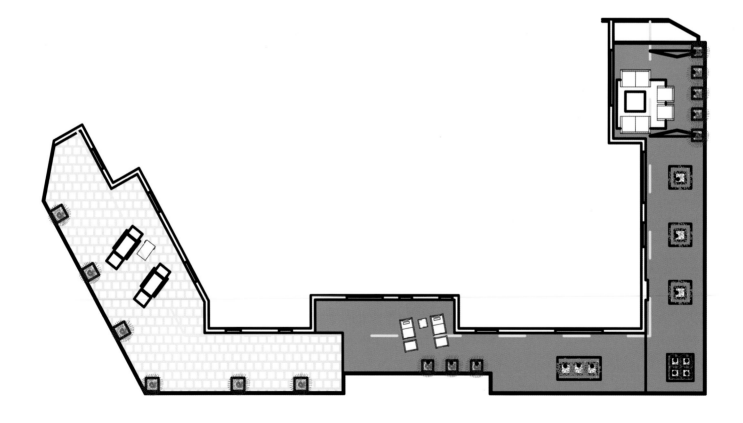

The design was based on the owners'
requirement of simple maintenance:
synthetic wood, a reduced number of
hardy plant varieties, light but elegant
furniture, and a lamp made of PE.

The original furnishings allow lights to be installed inside them to create a warm and elegant atmosphere, particularly at night. Spotlights positioned inside the plant pots illuminate the beautiful shrubs.

At dusk, the sun gives way to the glow of artificial light that fills the night with magic.

CHARMING SPACES

FLOORING/PAVING: Brazilian walnut tropical hardwood decking and white marble pebbles.

PLANT POTS AND PLANTER BOXES: Planter boxes in Brazilian walnut.

FURNISHINGS: Cantilever bench in Brazilian walnut.

PLANT SPECIES: *Magnolia grandiflora gallisoniensis, Trachelospermum jasminoides,* grasses, *Olea Europaea,* and *Hedera helix.*

Besides remodeling the inside of this protected historic building dating from last century, the client decided to make better use of the exterior space. The project consisted of building a terrace over an indoor swimming pool and gymnasium, and a garden at the entrance to the property. The outstanding feature of the terrace is the cantilever bench made from Brazilian walnut. It serves a double purpose as a seat and also as an improvised table for a light meal. This space is accessed from the garden at the entrance and also from the module housing the gym and pool.

Of note in the work done to the garden is the mix of different materials used as paving: white marble pebbles, Brazilian walnut wood strips, and stamped concrete tiles. The landscape designers arranged a variety of plants at the edges of this space so as not to break the visual effect created by the different materials.

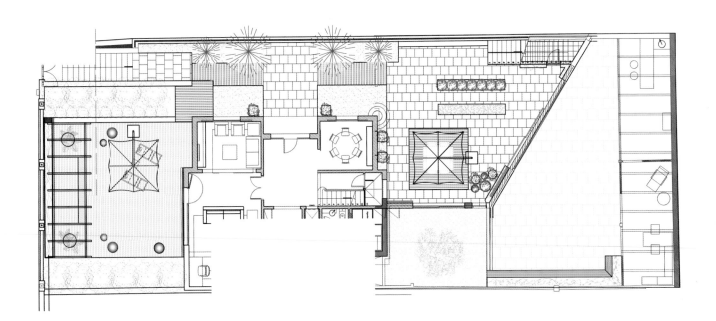

By means of combining three different types of materials (white stones, wooden strips and stamped concrete) in the pavement, both integration and separation of the spaces were achieved at the same time.

The bench was built from the same material as the decking. This piece has a double function as it serves as a seat (for resting or reading, for example) and as a table for a light meal.

A SPACE TO ENJOY THE SUN AND THE GENTLE BREEZE DURING THE WARMEST MONTHS.

MAKING THE MOST OF SPACE

FLOORING/PAVING: Gray WPC and Bolon Ethnic Collection woven vinyl flooring.

PLANT POTS AND PLANTER BOXÉS: Charcoal gray rotomolded PE plant pots and gray WPC planter boxes.

FURNISHINGS: Gray WPC chill out sofa and cushions covered in marine-grade fabric.

PLANT SPECIES: *Phoenix robellini, Ficus benjamina,* and *Viburnum lucidum.*

LIGHTING: Tegola stainless steel wall lamp and Nautilus directional spotlights with ground spike.

With the increasing importance people place on free time in today's world, balconies are greatly appreciated. Located on a high rise building in Barcelona, this small balcony was designed as the external prolongation of the living area and is the highlight of the home.

The clients wanted a space where they could unwind from the stress of the day and enjoy their peace in private. This desire was brought to life with the creation of a chill out space where privacy was protected by means of the planting of small shrubs to form a natural fence. Besides providing privacy, the height of the vegetation allows the city views to be enjoyed.

A large L-shaped sofa was positioned on a platform built of PWC painted gray. The flooring and furnishings were made using the same composite wood material, and white marine-grade fabric was chosen for the cushions.

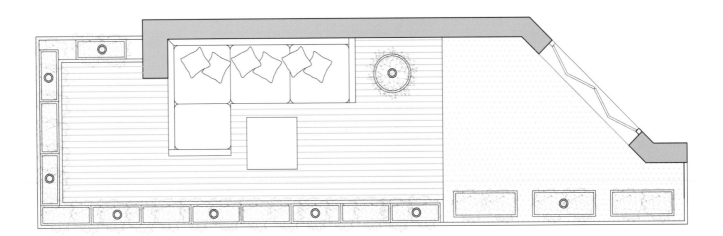

To protect privacy and allow in the greatest amount of natural light, two of the main aims of the project, several blinds were installed that can be raised and lowered as required.

THE RIGHT TOUCH OF INSPIRATION HAS TURNED THIS LITTLE SPACE INTO THE MOST TREASURED PART OF THE HOME.

LIVING WATER

FLOORING/PAVING: Brazilian walnut tropical hardwood decking and white marble pebbles.

PLANT POTS AND PLANTER BOXES: White rotomolded PE plant pots and Brazilian walnut wood planter boxes.

FURNISHINGS: Brazilian walnut wood bench and acrylic-covered cushions.

The materials and colors used in the flooring, furnishings, plant pots, and planter boxes when creating this balcony are perfectly integrated with the walls of the building. The horizontal lines of the wooden strips form a balanced combination with the horizontal rows of bricks on the wall.

This balcony was designed as if it were a rooftop terrace. The atmosphere of tranquillity is enhanced by the sound of water coming from a weathered steel fountain. Worked by a pump, the water is raised to the soffit from where it falls into a rectangular base. The floor below this base was turned into a mantle of white marble pebbles. In front of this structure, two spherical lamps, each with a candle inside, give off a gentle glow at night.

Seats by the large windows and on wooden support frames are graced with a number of cushions for added comfort. Tropical hardwood was used in the other pieces of furniture: two sofas, a small table, and a large, long planter box where trees reach a perfect height to protect privacy.

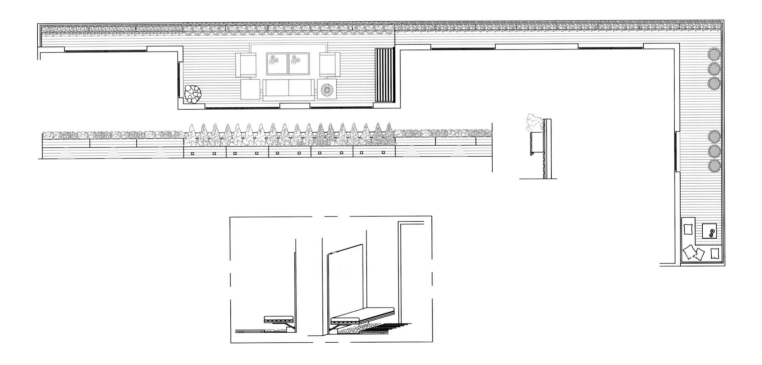

The weathered steel fountain is the feature of this unique space. The sound of water washing over the seemingly rusted soffit, produces a relaxing effect.

PLACID MOMENTS OF REST TO THE RHYTHM OF THE GENTLY MURMURING WATER IN THE FOUNTAIN.

INSIDE BALCONY OR OUTDOOR LIVING ROOM?

FLOORING/PAVING: Brazilian walnut tropical hardwood decking.

PLANT POTS AND PLANTER BOXES: Plant pots made from white lacquered plastic, and custom-made treated pine planter boxes.

FURNISHINGS: Synthetic rattan sofas and polyester-covered cushions, aluminum table with teak top, chairs and sunloungers in aluminum and Batyline mesh.

PLANT SPECIES: *Olea europaea*, *Citrus* trees, *Schefflera*, *Howea fosteriana*, *Cycas revoluta*, and *Euphorbia*.

LIGHTING: 360-degree directional die-cast aluminum halogen spotlights, stainless steel recessed spotlights, and rotomolded PE standing lamp.

This roof terrace on the top floor of a building is comprised of three perfectly defined spaces with different uses: a solarium, an outdoor eating area, and an exterior living area. The living area is formed by a porch covered by a frame structure made with walnut-stained pine wood and wood faced with tiles for waterproofing. The outdoor eating area features a pergola with a frame similar to that of the porch, but differentiated by the retractable awning system comprising polyester screen shades. The solarium has two aluminum sunloungers and an outside freestanding shower featuring a Brazilian walnut wood post.

The most striking thing about the terrace and its perfectly defined spaces is the furniture, made with aluminum and synthetic rattan. From their appearance, these furnishings would be more appropriate inside the dwelling, but their originality is precisely to be found in their setting. This terrace is a good example of how to project the interior of a home to the space outside.

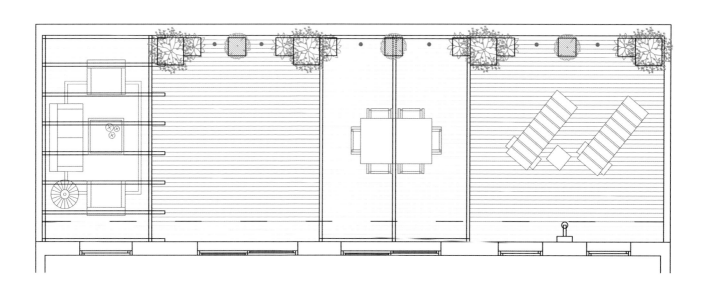

The unique feature of this project is the combination of three zones in a single space: solarium, living area, and eating area. The last of these is installed under a wooden pergola, an awning of waves, and a number of screen shades.

The owners' plants were made good use of by placing them strategically in front of the railings of this large terrace. A certain amount of privacy was achieved in this way.

OUTDOOR LIVING THAT ALLOWS CITY LIFE TO BE CONTEMPLATED BUT AWAY FROM CURIOUS ONLOOKERS.

PLANT SCULPTURE

FLOORING/PAVING: Gray WPC decking.

PLANT POTS AND PLANTER BOXES: Charcoal gray rotomolded PE plant pots and custom-made gray WPC planter boxes.

FURNISHINGS: Gray WPC chill out sofa, cushions covered in marine-grade fabric, aluminum and acrylic patio umbrella with a concrete base, aluminum and Batyline mesh sunlounger, and coal-fired grill with side table.

PLANT SPECIES: Macro bonsai *Ficus nitida*, *Cupressus sempervirens*, *Cycas revoluta*, *Washingtonia*, *Olea europaea*, *Citrus limon*, *Citrus calamondin*, and *Punica granatum*.

LIGHTING: Stainless steel recessed spotlights and die-cast aluminum halogen spotlights.

The work of landscape designers at this single-family dwelling was centered on two spaces: the front entrance and the garden located at the rear. The project consisted of building an urban terrace in a garden facing the sea and surrounded by vegetation.

Before the project, there was an unused space at the entrance to the garden. The client wanted to give this a purely decorative aspect, so the designers had the idea of creating a plant sculpture. A more normal solution would have been to install a fountain or monolith, but the designers decided to plant a macro bonsai. A gray WPC planter box matching the main colors of the façade was put in position. A mantle of white stones was laid over it and grass was planted around the tree.

The highlight of the rear garden is the chill out space. This area was covered with the same wood as the entrance and a pool deck was built. This area features a long bench with cushions of different colors and an aluminum patio umbrella.

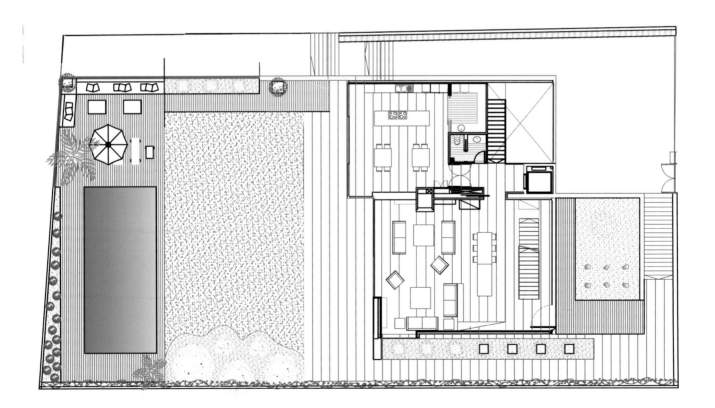

At the entrance to the garden, the landscape designers created a plant sculpture consisting of a macro bonsai arranged over a structure of gray-stained WPC serving as a planter box.

"Building a terrace in a garden" was the idea the designers made reality in this private family home. The elderly owners were not interested in a solarium, but prefered a chill out space where they could spend pleasant evenings.

Sculpted nature welcomes visitors to a large garden from where one can contemplate the immenseness of the sea.

ARTFUL VIEWS

FLOORING/PAVING: Brazilian walnut tropical hardwood decking.

PLANT POTS AND PLANTER BOXES: High quality plastic Lechuza plant pots painted metallic gray and custom-made Brazilian walnut wood planter boxes.

FURNISHINGS: White PE and aluminum sunloungers by Gandia Blasco, white synthetic-fiber modular sofa, acrylic-covered cushions, Round by Cristophe Pillet painted steel table and high chairs.

PLANT SPECIES: *Citrus limon, Ficus benjamina, Phoenix roebelenii, Laurus nobilis* and *Eugenia.*

LIGHTING: Adjustable spotlights with stems and rotomolded PE standing lamp.

The unbeatable location of this penthouse, in a district featuring several historic landmarks, required a design that was respectful with the views. In order to achieve this, it was decided to position the plants at the ends of the terrace, not by the balustrade. This enabled privacy to be maintained without interfering with the ability to contemplate the artistic surrounds. Plastic plant pots decorated with metallic paint were used.

The decking comprises long boards of Brazilian walnut to provide the setting with a visual pattern. Two spaces were created on the terrace: a solarium and a bar. The chill out space features a table and two high chairs in painted steel. The solarium is furnished with two white PE and aluminum sunloungers and a modular sofa with chaise longue. White is the dominant color in both décor and furnishings, providing a touch of elegance and minimalism to the setting.

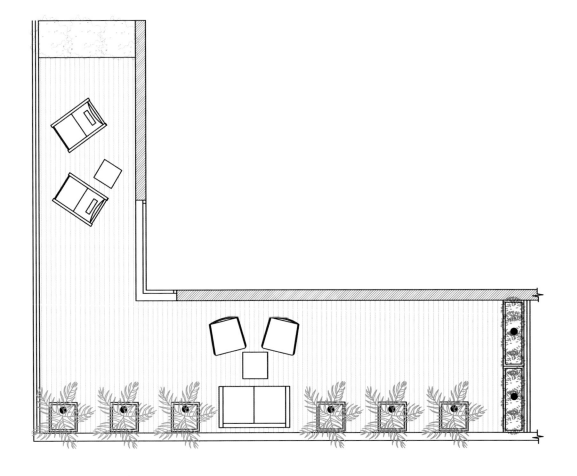

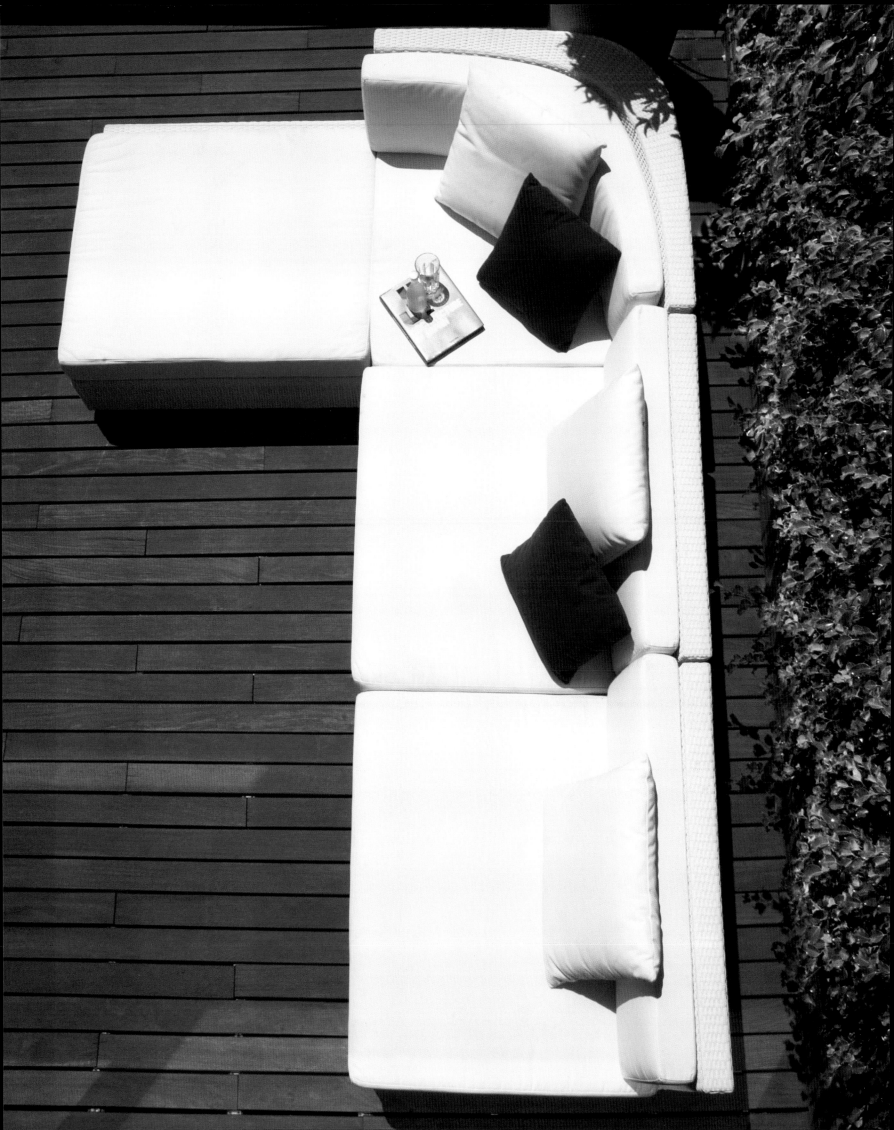

The bar space is located at one end of the terrace over a platform made of wooden strips, and features a square table and two high chairs.

The client's top priority was to maintain the views from the terrace. In keeping with this, the designers did not use any elements that would block the view of the surrounding landmarks.

The essence of Modernism impregnates the clean lines of this terrace and creates a unique fusion.

OUTDOOR LIVING

FLOORING/PAVING: Brazilian walnut tropical hardwood decking and white marble pebbles.

PLANT POTS AND PLANTER BOXES: Charcoal gray rotomolded PE plant pots and custom-made Brazilian walnut planter box.

FURNISHINGS: Synthetic fiber sofa with acrylic-covered cushions, synthetic fiber dining chairs with acrylic-covered cushions, aluminum and glass table, and aluminum and PE daybed with mattress upholstered in marine-grade fabric.

PLANT SPECIES: *Viburnum lucidum*, *Cycas revoluta* and *Punica granatum*.

LIGHTING: 360-degree directional die-cast aluminum halogen spotlights and resin standing and table lamps.

This project is found on the grounds of a single-family dwelling and involves the garden at the entrance to the house, which has been given the design of an urban terrace. The project consisted of the construction of a walkway in Brazilian walnut tropical hardwood leading from the gates of the property to the house. Large plant pots with trees and plants were arranged over white stones on both sides of the walkway. A large pergola was also built using 2.6 x 2.6 ft tubes in anodized aluminum with a rustproof finish. This structure is covered with a retractable wave awning that allows the area under it to become a solarium when opened, or a chill out space when closed. Two sofas and a daybed were placed inside this space. A stainless steel fountain was positioned at one end for a purely ornamental effect, while the other end features an eating area and grill. One of the main aims of this project was to move activities that normally take place indoors, such as cooking, eating, and resting, outdoors.

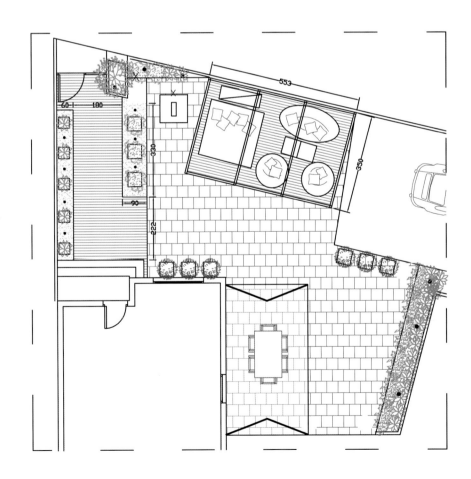

The terrace is the space where the interior and exterior of a home are brought together. This case shows the great versatility a space of this nature offers, as it can be used as a place of relaxation, for sunbathing, or even as an open-air dining area.

The highlights of this terrace are the wood
used in the walkway and chill out space,
the concrete paving the rest of the terrace,
and water, which serves as a decorative
element.

Versatility and function merged in a single setting removed from the noise of the city.

EXOTIC TOUCH

FLOORING/PAVING: Brazilian walnut hardwood decking and white marble pebbles.

PLANT POTS AND PLANTER BOXES: Black and white lacquered plastic plant pots.

FURNISHINGS: Sunloungers and chairs in aluminum and Batyline mesh, aluminum and teak tables.

PLANT SPECIES: *Citrus* trees, *Buxus sempervirens*, *Ficus nitida* and *Schefflera*.

LIGHTING: Stainless steel recessed spotlights.

Located on the highest floor of a single-family home, this original roof terrace creates three clearly distinct spaces in one. An eating area covered by an awning is found closest to the dwelling. A wooden platform was built at one of the ends of the terrace where a table and four chairs are arranged near a structure housing a whirlpool bath. This structure shows distinct Asian influence and replaces the typical daybed. At the other end of the terrace is an area with two sunloungers that serves as a solarium. The wooden decking allows the relaxation areas to be separated from the eating area.

Vegetation was planted in large pots of different sizes resting over white marble pebbles. The lighting was designed to enhance the plants, and to create a warm and tranquil atmosphere. This effect was achieved by installing recessed spotlights in the wooden floor and pots.

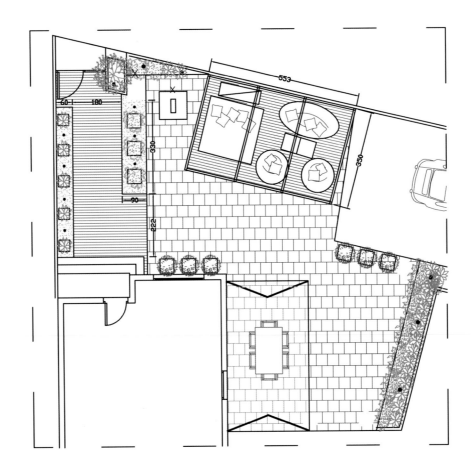

This terrace is divided into three areas: a
covered eating area under an awning, an
open space over a platform incorporating
a whirlpool bath and a solarium.

A LITTLE ASIAN LUXURY THAT MAINTAINS A HIGHLY-PRIZED MEDITERRANEAN ESSENCE.

STAIRWAY TO HEAVEN

FLOORING/PAVING: Autoclave-treated Flanders pine, stained white, and white marble pebbles.

PLANT POTS AND PLANTER BOXES: High quality plastic plant pots, lacquered white.

FURNISHINGS: Chill out divans in Flanders pine stained white, armchair and sofa with frame in anodized aluminum and PE, daybed with frame in anodized aluminum and PE, cushions and mattresses upholstered in marine-grade fabric, coffee and dining tables in anodized aluminum and PE, chair in aluminum and Batyline mesh.

PLANT SPECIES: *Phoenix roebelenii, Cycas revoluta* and *Phoenix canariensis*.

LIGHTING: Stainless steel recessed spotlights and INOU rotomolded PE standing lamp and ceiling light fixture.

One of the greatest challenges of this project was integrating the different levels created when building a swimming pool on the roof of a high-rise building. Rooftop swimming pools are built on a raised platform and create levels that are different than the other spaces. This split level was made use of as the back of a long seat in the chill out space at one of the ends of the pool. A solarium was placed on the other side, with access to the pool from here by a series of steps.

One of the most prominent aspects of this project is that the wooden decking is stained white. This combines perfectly with the marine-grade fabrics found on the armchair, sofa, daybeds, cushions and mattresses. The installation of a retractable wave awning means the chill out space can be covered. Standing out also is the pergola covered with pine wood slats over the large dining table and eight chairs.

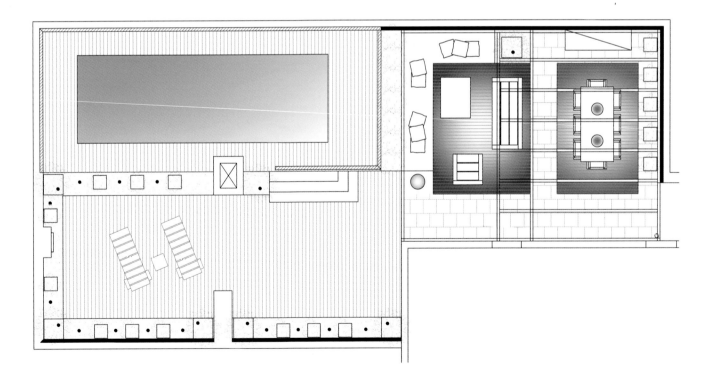

Its original shape, the predominant use of wood in the different spaces, and the stair rail made from unbreakable glass make this rooftop a spectacular space.

Despite the swimming pool being on a higher level than the other spaces, the urban landscape can be enjoyed from anywhere on this terrace.

A MAGNIFICENT SWIMMING POOL CROWNS THIS SPACE WHERE TIME SEEMS TO STAND STILL.

MINI PARADISE

FLOORING/PAVING: Brazilian walnut decking.

PLANT POTS AND PLANTER BOXES: White lacquered plastic plant pots and walnut-stained pine planter boxes.

FURNISHINGS: Brazilian walnut chill out sofa, cushions covered in marine-grade fabric, table and bench in anodized aluminum with ceramic tops, rotomolded PE chair, sunloungers in aluminum and Batyline mesh, and aluminum and acrylic patio umbrella.

PLANT SPECIES: *Buxus sempervirens rotundifolia, Cycas revoluta* and *Olea europaea*.

LIGHTING: Stainless steel recessed spotlights in the decking and directional die-cast aluminum spotlights for planter boxes.

The patio of a single-family home was divided to create three different spaces: a solarium with swimming pool, an eating area, and a chill out space. Despite the small size of the patio, the client wanted a pool built. An above-ground swimming pool with an aluminum frame was built and a stained pine wood deck was built around it. A freestanding shower with a Brazilian walnut post was erected on one corner of the deck. To protect the privacy required in this type of space, stained pine fences were built at different heights. High quality synthetic lawn was laid in the solarium as it requires little maintenance. In the chill out area a long sofa was placed with a base made form the same material as the pool deck.

An aluminum and acrylic patio umbrella was installed in the eating area under which is a rectangular table with room to seat four people or more. Different plant varieties were strategically planted: the smallest in wooden planter boxes and the largest in plastic pots.

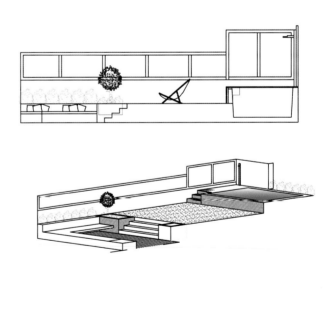

The main objective of this project was to install a mini swimming pool in a small patio with different levels and for it to be perfectly integrated with the other spaces.

On an uneven site, the synthetic lawn and wood help to define and separate the different spaces (solarium, pool, and eating area).

Visual harmony in a small space with different areas offering maximum enjoyment.

LEISURE SPACE

FLOORING/PAVING: Brazilian walnut wood decking and fence, Brazilian redwood fence, and white marble pebbles.

PLANT POTS AND PLANTER BOXES: White lacquered plastic plant pots and Brazilian walnut planter boxes.

FURNISHINGS: Chill out sofa in Brazilian walnut, cushions covered in marine-grade fabric, table in aluminum with Compact top, chairs and sunloungers in aluminum and Batyline mesh.

PLANT SPECIES: *Olea europaea*, *Citrus limon*, *Pittosporum tobira nana*, *Thuja aurea* and *Eugenia*.

LIGHTING: Directional die-cast aluminum spotlights and stainless steel recessed spotlights

One of the challenges of the project was turning a rooftop terrace into a multi-purpose space. The spaces were clearly separated and differentiated through the erection of shade structures. A pergola with a retractable wave awning, a few sunloungers, and aluminum side tables make up the solarium. This pergola is connected to another structure with a permanent pergola made from slats of Brazilian walnut and Plexiglas. In the space below this pergola is a dining table with room for six people.

A bench for resting on was built to take advantage of the different levels created by the fences. Opposite this a freestanding shower was installed with a post of treated and stained wood. The last space is a play area with a special stainless steel outdoor foosball table, a portable gas grill, and a city-style bench. The designers decided to leave the original paving but left their mark with the placement of white pebbles under the bench.

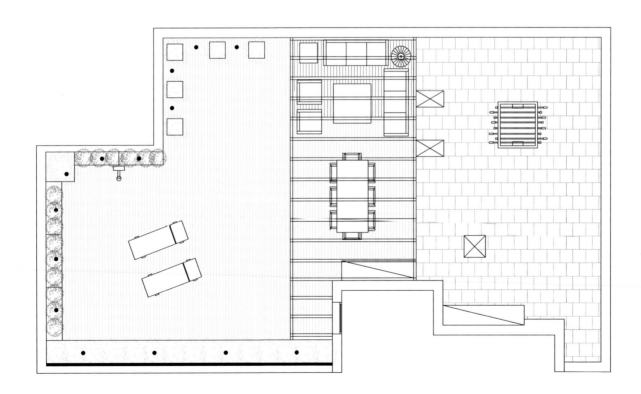

The large dimensions of this terrace allowed the creation of different spaces with multiple uses. At one of the ends a pergola with retractable screen shades allows the space to be turned into a solarium or a place for relaxation.

The walls of exposed brickwork and plants of considerable height are a practical and appealing solution to protect the privacy of the terrace users.

Multiple leisure spaces to satisfy needs in times of stress.

OUTDOOR EATING

FLOORING/PAVING: Brazilian walnut decking and fence and travertine tile paving.

PLANT POTS AND PLANTER BOXES: Rotomolded PE plant pots.

FURNISHINGS: Synthetic rattan sofas with polyester cushions, stainless steel dining table with teak top, plastic Phantom chairs, sunloungers in aluminum and Batyline mesh, and mattresses upholstered in marine-grade fabric.

PLANT SPECIES: *Magnolia grandiflora gallisoniensis, Citrus limon, Viburnum lucidum, Prunus cerasifera pissardi, Trachelospermum jasminoides, Buxus* and *Eugenia*.

LIGHTING: 360-degree directional die-cast aluminum spotlights and stainless steel recessed spotlights.

The project was designed for the patio of a single-family home. The owners wanted an outdoor eating area and a small swimming pool. A space was set aside next to the pool for a solarium with Brazilian walnut hardwood decking and two integrated mattresses upholstered in marine-grade fabric. The poolside area was tiled in travertine marble and as small table with plastic Phantom chairs was placed on one of the sides.

The outdoor eating area is at one of the ends of the patio, under a pergola made of autoclave-treated laminated pine stained walnut brown. The roof of the pergola, made of natural wicker and panels of Plexiglas, is a feature with great originality. The same kind of furnishings were used in this area as for the poolside area. The porch between the house and the patio was turned into a relaxation area and works to unite the two spaces. A number of large, inviting sofas were arranged here for guests to rest on.

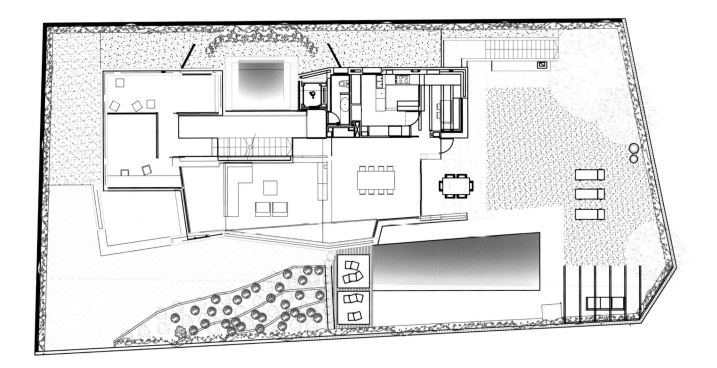

A feature of this patio is the wooden decking adjoining the pool. Two mattresses were integrated into the deck for sunbathing and form the most unique element of the project.

A suitable solution for this type of patio is to create a space with plentiful vegetation; however, the landscape designers created different spaces with the goal of allowing "the outside to be enjoyed from inside".

DELIGHTFUL GATHERINGS AROUND A TABLE PROTECTED FROM THE SUN UNDER A PERGOLA THAT LETS THE BREEZE
PASS THROUGH.

SPORTING SPIRIT

FLOORING/PAVING: Brazilian walnut tropical hardwood decking and white marble pebbles.

FURNISHINGS: Brazilian walnut chill out sofa, cushions covered in marine-grade fabric, and a sunlounger in aluminum and Batyline mesh.

PLANT SPECIES: *Citrus aurantium, Ophiopogon* and *Hedera helix.*

LIGHTING: Stainless steel light fixtures recessed in the decking, directional die-cast aluminum spotlights and a cube lamp in rotomolded PE.

This house is in the midst of the city and features a long courtyard patio which was originally used as an external access. The client wanted to build a large pool for swimming in. This requirement led the landscape designers to adapt the rectangular pool to this reduced space. They positioned the pool as closely as possible to one of the ends of the patio, which allowed them to build a walkway in Brazilian walnut hardwood and to lay an area with white marble pebbles.

The existing plants were maintained on both sides of the rectangular space to serve a double function: to protect privacy and to provide the necessary effect of green and coolness in a space of these characteristics. Where the ground level changes between the house and the patio, a chill out sofa was built from the same material as the pool deck – Brazilian walnut. The difference in level was also made use of to install steps to the pool and a number of wooden planter boxes.

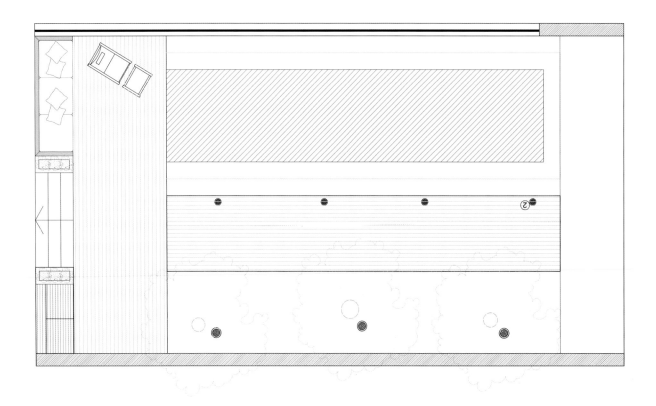

The element conditioning the design of this courtyard patio was the pool; the owners wanted a rectangular pool for swimming, a space with vegetation, and an area for relaxing and sunbathing.

An escape for the mind is provided by submerging in this placid, private space, while the body is soothed by the water.

PLANT-FREE TERRACE

FLOORING/PAVING: Decking in synthetic Brazilian walnut colored wood, wooden fences in synthetic Brazilian walnut colored wood and white marble pebbles.

PLANT POTS AND PLANTER BOXES: High quality plastic Lechuza plant pots, lacquered in off white.

FURNISHINGS: Table with aluminum frame and teak top, chairs in enameled aluminum and Batyline mesh, chill out sofa in synthetic Brazilian walnut colored wood and cushions covered in marine-grade fabric.

LIGHTING: 360-degree directional die-cast aluminum spotlights.

It was decided that all vegetation would be done away with in this courtyard patio. The only note of green in the project would be provided by a small planter box located in the transition space between the dwelling and the patio. The project basically involved creating a terrace in the limited space of a small courtyard.

Synthetic wood was used for the deck, the furniture and the enclosures to protect the privacy of the terrace. A covered outdoor eating area was designed for the space adjoining the dwelling with a pergola structure made from 0.26 x 0.26 ft tubes in anodized aluminum. The roof was made from pine wood stained the color of Brazilian walnut and Plexiglas panels.

A series of terraced steps was built to give access to the swimming pool, together with a chill out sofa to separate the leisure space from the eating area. Decorative elements are provided by the cushions covered in marine-grade fabric with printed plant shapes to compensate the absence of vegetation in this project.

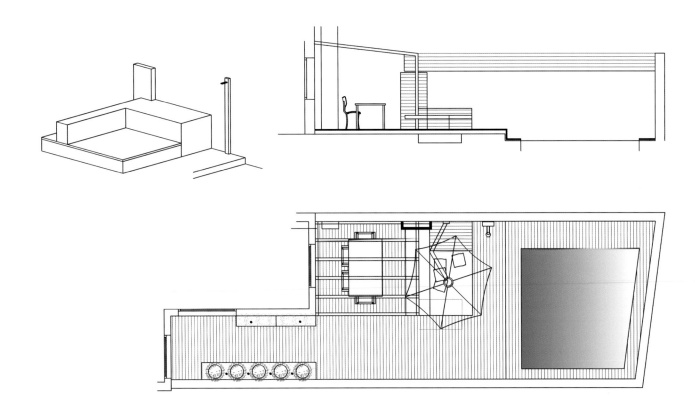

The appearance of wood gives exterior spaces an austere and minimalist feel, which can appreciated in this contemporary terrace.

The area closest to the dwelling features a pergola with an aluminum frame and wooden roof that serves as an outdoor eating area. Synthetic wood was used for the decking and furnishings alike.

The colors of earth and wood bathed in sunlight bring a feeling of warmth to this setting of infinite serenity.

BIG CHILL OUT

FLOORING/PAVING: Brazilian walnut wood decking, white marble pebbles, and Brazilian redwood fence.

PLANT POTS AND PLANTER BOXES: Rotomolded PE plant pots and Brazilian walnut wood planter boxes.

FURNISHINGS: Brazilian walnut wood chill out sofa and cushions covered in marine-grade fabric.

LIGHTING: Directional die-cast aluminum halogen spotlights.

Terraces and balconies play an essential role in architecture. In a sense, they represent the continuation of a dwelling in the open air. This project is a clear example of how this occurs. The roof terrace is larger than the dwelling, so the clients decided to extend the floor space of their home outside. A summer eating area was located under a pergola structure with a frame of aluminum tubes and a roof of Brazilian walnut slate and panels of matte glass. The walls are also of aluminum and glass. Sliding doors allow the eating area to be hermetically sealed in winter and opened up in summer.

Brazilian walnut hardwood was used for the decking, furnishings, and planter boxes. A large sofa was positioned in one of the corners with upholstery and cushion covers in marine-grade fabric. The privacy of this chill out space is protected by the installation of wooden fences and varieties of plants like olive trees.

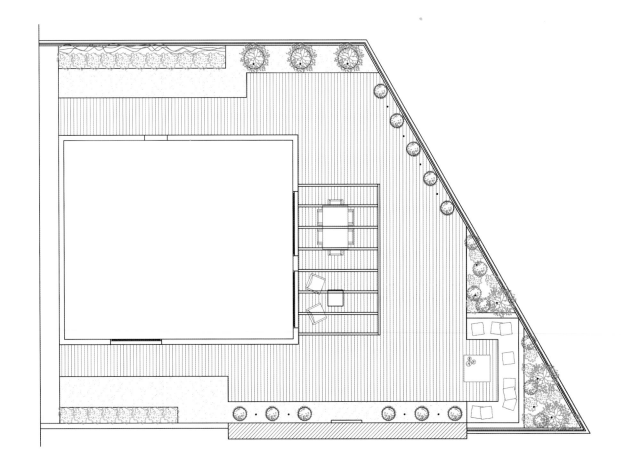

A chill out space was created at one of the ends of this enormous roof terrace. Here a U-shaped seating system was installed with a wooden frame and marine-grade fabric upholstery.

TWO PRIVILEGED SPACES WITH AN INVITING ELEGANCE FOR GATHERINGS IN A RELAXED ATMOSPHERE.

GARDEN TERRACE

FLOORING/PAVING: Brazilian walnut tropical hardwood decking and walnut-stained Flanders pine fence.

FURNISHINGS: Sofa and coffee table in synthetic fiber with acrylic-covered cushions, teak wood dining table and chairs, rattan ottoman, synthetic fiber sunloungers with acrylic-covered cushions, synthetic fiber table and chairs, daybed with marine-grade fabric upholstered mattress.

LIGHTING: Die-cast aluminum halogen spotlights, rotomolded PE standing lamps, and stainless steel lamps.

This garden is part of a house in a residential subdivision. Pools are normally designed to take advantage of the width of plot; however, in this case it was decided to position it lengthways so that the owners could use it for swimming. The layout of spaces is somewhat unconventional. If it is common to position a pergola near the façade of a house and locate a swimming pool and solarium after this, the designers did the total opposite.

Three distinct spaces were laid out under the L-shaped pergola: an outdoor eating area, a chill out sofa, and a daybed. The pergola has a structural frame made from 0.26 x 0.26 ft cm anodized aluminum tubes and a roof made of walnut-stained Flanders pine wood slats over the eating area, and Plexiglas panels over the two other areas. Wood decking was used for the poolside area and the and the pergola space.

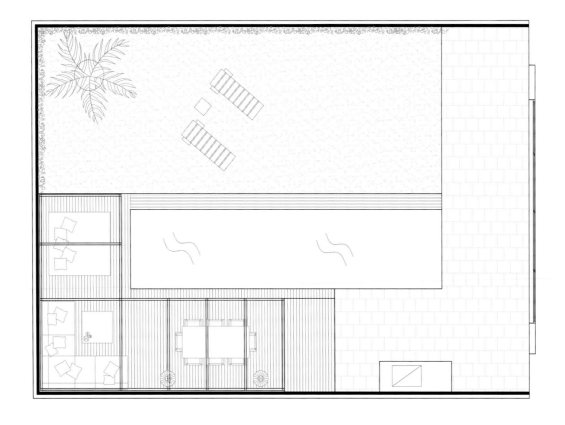

The originality of this project comes from the unconventional layout of spaces. If it is more common to position canopies near a house and a wide pool near the perimeter enclosure, this project sees the long pool located near the house and the canopies adjacent to the perimeter wall.

Most of the lighting in this garden was
installed in the pool, taking advantage of its
large size. Small light fixtures and candles
were also placed in the pergola area.

THIS PRIVATE CITY GARDEN OOZES RIVIERA GLAMOUR AND SOPHISTICATION.

ORIGINAL ROOF

FLOORING/PAVING: Brazilian walnut wood decking, white and gray marble pebbles, and Brazilian redwood fence.

PLANT POTS AND PLANTER BOXES: Black and white rotomolded PE plant pots.

FURNISHINGS: Synthetic fiber sofa with acrylic-covered cushions, stainless steel dining table with teak top, stainless steel and Batyline mesh chairs.

LIGHTING: 360-degree directional die- cast aluminum halogen spotlights and rotomolded PE standing lamps.

This project involved the front, side and rear gardens of a townhouse. A line of spotlights was installed along a wooden walkway connecting the front gate with the dwelling. Gray and white marble pebbles line both sides of the walkway forming a surface mantle on which plant pots were placed with different plant varieties. A wooden deck was built on the side of the plot with a number of sunloungers, and a summer eating area was located at the rear. The table seats six and is partially shaded by a screen pergola that serves as an awning and which can be removed if required.

One of the most original features of this project is the pergola adjoining the house. The owner, a designer by profession, wanted the wooden slats of the roof perpendicular to the length, instead of parallel, as is habitual, to create an original effect of light and shade. A large synthetic fiber sofa with acrylic-covered cushions was placed under the pergola–interior furnishing located outdoors on this occasion.

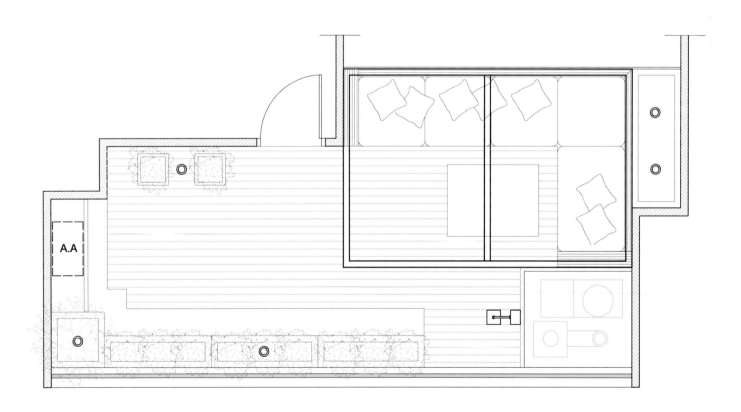

This project is a good example of how an outdoor space can be given an indoors feel through the use of furniture that is normally placed in the interior.

One of the most unusual elements of this project is the pergola roof. The wooden slats are arranged perpendicularly instead of lengthways.

The walkway is an invitation to discover the home; on the other side is a space to delight the senses.

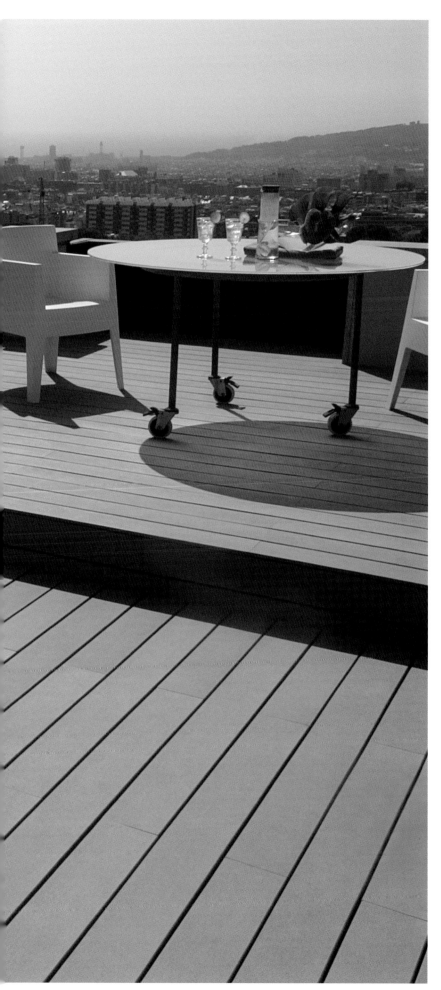

SPECTACULAR LOOKOUT
WITH SEA VIEWS

FLOORING/PAVING: Gray WPC decking.

FURNISHINGS: Aluminum and PE sunloungers with cushions covered in marine-grade fabric.

LIGHTING: Rotomolded PE ball.

This wooden deck is located on a roof terrace of a single-family home built on the side of a mountain. The terrace offers magnificent views and serves as a lookout over the city. Glass panels were installed as a rail to protect against the wind and to guarantee safety.

The change in level on the site was taken advantage of for a swimming pool. This split level also allowed different spaces to be created at different heights. The space nearest to the pool was made into a first solarium with aluminum and PE sunloungers. Terraced steps lead to a second solarium, and to a space away from the pool where a round table and two chairs invite one to relax.

The predominant material of this project is gray WPC, which is used to integrate the different spaces and levels in particular. Planting of different vegetation types was not necessary for this project as the terrace was designed for observing the nature surrounding the house.

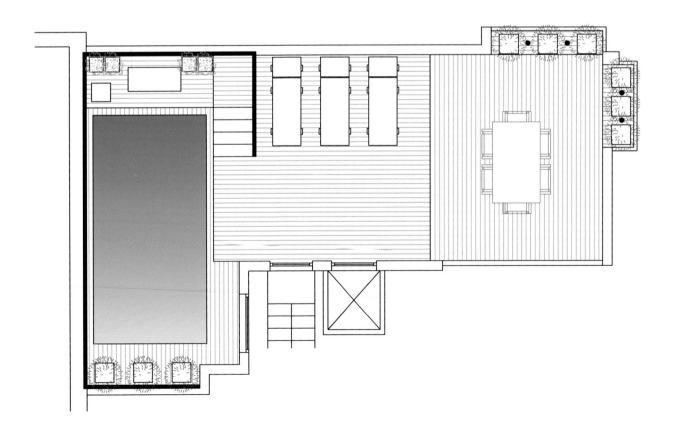

The terrace is surrounded by abundant vegetation, leading the designers to do away with plants. The uneven nature of the site allowed the terrace to become a lookout.

THE CITY GOES ON FOREVER BELOW YOU, THE GREEN OF THE MOUNTAINS CONTRASTS WITH THE CLEAN AND SIMPLE LINES OF THE TERRACE.

URBAN SHIP DECK

FLOORING/PAVING: Brazilian walnut tropical hardwood decking.

PLANT POTS AND PLANTER BOXES: White rotomolded PE plant pots and Brazilian walnut wood planter boxes.

PLANT SPECIES: *Citrus limon, Rosmarinus officinalis* and *Bougainvillea.*

This wide split-level terrace rises over the rooftops of the city recalling the deck of a ship with its horizontal lines and the use of wood. An above-ground pool with an aluminum frame was installed on the highest part. Its surrounding deck was widened and is used as a solarium. The area below a wooden pergola shelters an oval table, creating a space that can be used for eating in summer or used an area for relaxation.

Brazilian walnut hardwood was used for floors, walls, and on the pergola. The height of the fence is greatest in the bathing area than in the rest, allowing privacy to be protected, while preserving views over the city. Different varieties of vegetation were planted in individual plant pots positioned around the sides of the terrace. A mantle of white marble pebbles was created in one of the corners of this space.

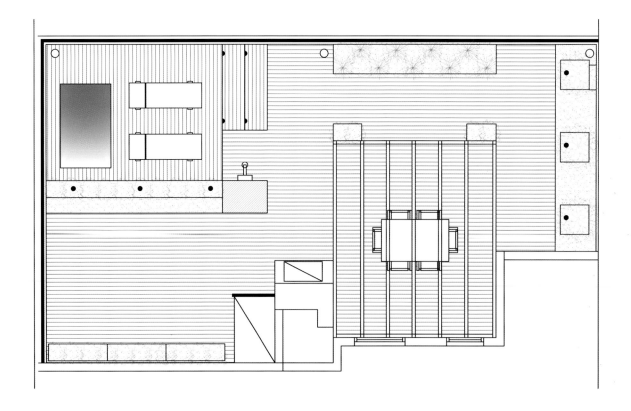

This roof terrace of an urban penthouse apartment makes use of wood as its single design element. Wood is present in the decking, structures, walls, planter boxes and furnishings.

URBAN SIMPLICITY AND EXOTIC MATERIALS — A SPECIAL HARMONY OF CONTRASTS ON THE ROOF.

GARDEN TURNED INTO URBAN TERRACE

FLOORING/PAVING: Brazilian walnut tropical hardwood decking.

PLANT POTS AND PLANTER BOXES: Black rotomolded PE plant pots.

FURNISHINGS: Brazilian walnut chill out sofa with cushions covered in marine-grade fabric, dining table in aluminum with Compact top, chairs in aluminum and Batyline mesh, pergola sofas, table, and chairs in anodized aluminum and PE, anodized aluminum and PE sunloungers, aluminum and acrylic offset patio umbrella (directional with 360 degree turning), outdoor unit in Brazilian walnut with granite countertop.

PLANT SPECIES: *Olea europaea, Phyllostachys aurea, Phyllostachys viridis, Phyllostachys nigra* and *Viburnum lucidum.*

The garden connects directly with the landscape surrounding the home. A view can be framed or certain landscape elements recreated through plantings of certain species. In this project, the owners and landscape designers created this garden as if it were an urban terrace. The walls, decking and furnishings were designed in Brazilian walnut, as was the pool deck. One of the poolside areas features an immense, long sofa shielded from the sun by a portable patio umbrella, which allows the sun to be enjoyed when it is folded. The offset patio umbrella is made up of an aluminum frame and acrylic shade, and can turn 360 degrees. Several anodized aluminum and PE sunloungers are arranged on the remaining sides of the pool.

A porch was built onto the house as the location for a small summer eating area. There is also an eating area and a living area under a pergola. The pergola structure is made from Flanders pine wood and comprises a laminated glass roof and roller shades.

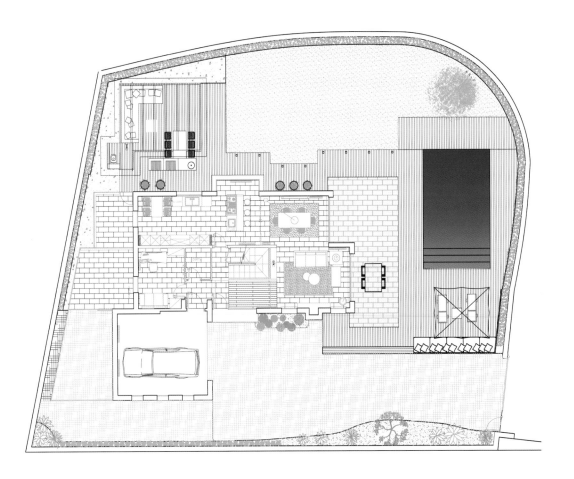

A chill out space was created at one of the ends of the pool deck. A large seating system is partially covered by a wide patio umbrella.

A WOODEN STAGE IN A GARDEN AND CORNERS LIKE A MOVIE SET WHERE ONE CAN DAYDREAM.

MINI PARADISE
CLOSE TO THE SEA

FLOORING/PAVING: Gray WPC decking and Bolon Ethnic Collection woven vinyl flooring.

FURNISHINGS: Aluminum and PE sofa, stainless steel and tinted glass dining table, chairs in stainless steel and Batyline mesh, anodized aluminum sunloungers with acrylic-covered cushions.

LIGHTING: Stainless steel recessed spotlights, directional die-cast aluminum halogen spotlights, rotomolded PE floating lamps, anodized aluminum and orange Plexiglas candle lamps, and rotomolded PE standing lamps.

Located practically on the edge of the sea, this garden with marvellous views was designed as an urban terrace. This large space features minimalist lines; only two simple pergola structures and partitions in the paving unifying this spacious surface can be observed. There is nothing to detract from the spectacular sea views.

The canopies are built from painted iron tubes and come complete with laminated glass roofs. Retractable awnings were installed under the glass and on the sides of the structures – roller screen shades. The pergola with the largest roof was designed to house a summer eating area with a table seating four; the second pergola houses a living area with sofas and a coffee table. An L-shaped pool was built with a pool deck. Plants were given only a token role: the lawn around the pool and a cypresses hedge around the enclosure. The lighting was chosen particularly to create an atmosphere of warmth and tranquillity.

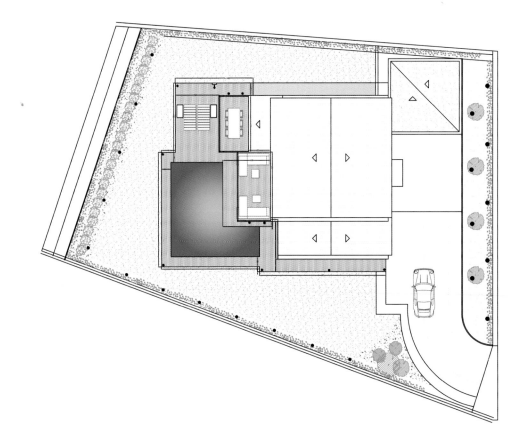

This garden was designed as if it were a terrace, a lookout over the sea. Two canopies adjoining the residence house an eating area and a living area, respectively.

Balance, relaxation and energy are merged to give enjoyment of magnificent Mediterranean views.

INDOOR OUTDOOR FUSION

FLOORING/PAVING: Brazilian walnut tropical hardwood decking and white marble pebbles.

PLANT POTS AND PLANTER BOXES: Bronze rotomolded PE plant pots.

FURNISHINGS: Armchair and ottoman with aluminum frame and Batyline mesh, acrylic-covered cushions, coffee table with aluminum frame and Compact top, dining table with aluminum frame and Compact top, chairs in aluminum and Batyline mesh, aluminum sunlounger with cushions covered in marine-grade fabric.

PLANT SPECIES: *Buxus sempervirens rotundifolia* and *Citrus*.

LIGHTING: Stainless steel recessed spotlights, directional die-cast aluminum spotlights, and painted iron standing lamps with Batyline mesh lampshade.

The whole home opens to the terrace, allowing interior and exterior spaces to merge. The floor to ceiling windows are elements integrating both spaces and allow abundant light into the residence. Raised at one end of the roof terrace is a small swimming pool. Wooden decking allows the other spaces to be integrated. Use was made of the height difference to create a solarium and install terraced steps to the pool.

The other spaces forming the terrace feature furnishings with a design that would be more common to see in the interior. Two examples of this are the lamps and the armchairs. A wall with plants was built on one side of the terrace to achieve the privacy required by the owners. Shrubs were planted in bronze rotomolded PE placed over a layer of pebbles.

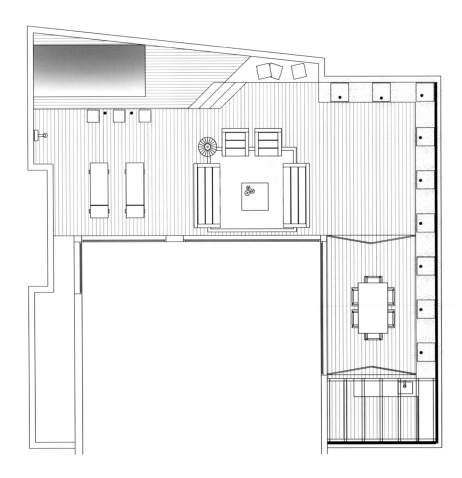

Rooftop swimming pools require raised
structures, which create different levels.
These can be compensated by the
construction of wooden steps or seats.

All of the furniture follows the same line of design. Furnishings were chosen for the exterior that could also be used inside the home. Vegetation was planted to help protect privacy.

THE SENSATION OF BEING IN AN INTERIOR SPACE IS INTERRUPTED BY THE SIGHT OF A FINE SHEET OF WATER.

CLEAN HORIZONTAL LINES

FLOORING/PAVING: Brazilian walnut tropical hardwood decking and white marble pebbles.

PLANT POTS AND PLANTER BOXES: Brazilian walnut tropical hardwood planter box.

FURNISHINGS: Custom-made chill out sofa in Brazilian walnut hardwood with cushions covered in marine-grade fabric, chairs in aluminum and Batyline mesh, tables in anodized aluminum with PE tops, daybed in aluminum and PE with mattress upholstered in marine-grade fabric.

PLANT SPECIES: *Viburnum lucidum*, *Eugenia*, *Olea europaea* and *Ficus benjamina*.

LIGHTING: 360-degree directional die-cast aluminum spotlights and stainless steel recessed spotlights.

This large terrace was totally created using wood, and clean horizontal lines predominate. This uniformity is only broken by the pebbles, which provide small touches of white.

The dwelling is divided into two clearly distinct zones: a space partially covered by an awning, and a totally open space. The former is a summer eating area, where the earth tones of the furniture were chosen to contrast with the dominant effect of the white in the latter. This open area is a chill out space, featuring a large L-shaped sofa, a small coffee table, and two aluminum deck chairs.

The landscape designers decided to place vegetation around the perimeter of the terrace. In one corner, just behind the chill out space, a large tree was planted to protect privacy. Shrubs were also planted so that city views could be preserved and enjoyed.

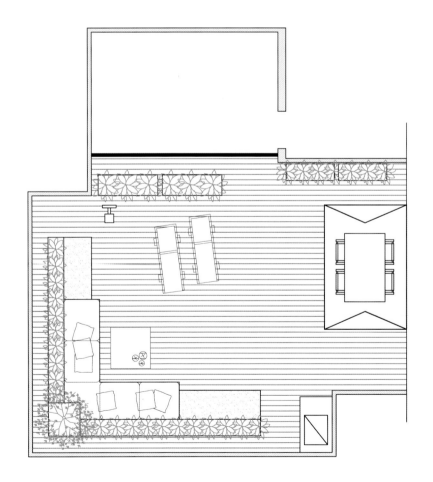

This urban roof terrace has vegetation planted around its perimeter. To protect privacy, the client preferred to have trees of medium height instead of installing a fence.

SENSORY SYMMETRY CREATED BY THE DECKING AND MINIMALIST FURNISHINGS DOMINATING THE SPACE.